X

W9-CFI-072

PALOS WEST LIBRARY
12700 South 104th Avenue
Palos Park, Ill. 60464

A ROOKIE READER™

KATIE COULDN'T

By Becky Bring McDaniel

Illustrations by Lois Axeman

Prepared under the direction of Robert Hillerich, Ph.D.

CHILDRENS PRESS ®

CHICAGO

To my mom and dad.

Library of Congress Cataloging in Publication Data

McDaniel, Becky Bring.
 Katie couldn't.

 (A Rookie Reader)
 Summary: Too little to ride a two-wheel bike or walk to
the park like her older brother and sister, Katie finds
there is something she can do that they cannot.
 [1. Size—Fiction. 2. Brothers and sisters—Fiction]
I. Title. II. Series.
PZ7.M478417Kar 1985 [E] 85-11666
ISBN 0-516-02069-2

Copyright © 1985 by Regensteiner Publishing Enterprises, Inc.
All rights reserved. Published simultaneously in Canada.
Printed in the United States of America.
  4 5 6 7 8 9 10 R 94 93 92 91 90 89 88 87

Jenny was the biggest. She could.
Kris was almost as big. He could.

3

Katie was little. She couldn't.

Jenny could ride a two wheel bike.

Kris could ride a two wheel bike.

Katie couldn't. She was little.

8

Kris could climb a high tree.
Jenny could climb a high tree.

Katie couldn't. She was little.

Jenny could stay up late at night.

Kris could stay up late at night.
Katie couldn't. She was little.

13

Kris could walk to the park.
Jenny could walk to the park.

PALOS WEST LIBRARY
12700 South 104th Avenue
Palos Park, Ill. 60464

15

Katie couldn't. She was little.

Jenny and Kris could do everything.

Katie couldn't. She was little.

Katie couldn't do this,

Katie couldn't do that.

Katie wondered what Katie could do.

22

Daddy came home from work,
and Jenny, Kris, and Katie ran
out to see him.

Daddy gave Jenny a hug.
He couldn't pick her up. She
was too big.

Daddy gave Kris a hug.
He couldn't pick him up. He
was too big.

Daddy picked Katie up and
tossed her up in the air.

Then he caught her and gave her a hug.

He could pick Katie up. She was little.

WORD LIST

a	Daddy	Kris	the
air	do	late	then
almost	everything	little	this
and	from	night	to
as	gave	out	too
at	he	park	tossed
big	her	pick	tree
biggest	high	picked	two
bike	him	ran	up
came	home	ride	walk
caught	hug	see	was
climb	in	she	what
could	Jenny	stay	wheel
couldn't	Katie	that	wondered
			work

About the Author

Becky Bring McDaniel was born in Ashland, Ohio but spent approximately half her life in Gainesville, Florida where she is pursuing a degree in creative writing at the University of Florida. Several of her poems have been published in such magazines as *Creative Years*, *The National Girl Scout Magazine*, and *Writers' Opportunities*. She is married and has three children ranging in ages from five to nine years old. She has several other manuscripts in progress and looks forward to a career in writing for children.

About the Artist

Lois Axeman was born and raised in Chicago, Illinois. She studied art in Chicago at the American Academy, Illinois Institute of Technology, and at the Art Institute. She taught illustration at the University of Illinois Circle Campus for four years. The mother of two grown children and grandmother of one, Lois and her husband, Harvey Retzloff, live on the fifty-fourth floor of a lakefront building where they both pursue their careers in the graphic arts. They share their home with their Shih Tzu dog Marty and their female cat Charlie. Lois uses her children, her grandchild, and her pets as models for her picture book characters. In their spare time Lois and Harvey enjoy painting, playing tennis, and growing orchids.

PALOS WEST LIBRARY
12700 South 104th Avenue
Palos Park, Ill. 60464

DATE DUE

MAY 04 1999 *10*			
NOV 15 2000			
FEB 25 2003	`		
MAR 12 2003			
APR 18 2003			
FEB 22 2005			
MAR 2 2005			

DEMCO 128-5046

02069-2

E
MCD

McDaniel, Becky Bring
Katie couldn't

$ 8.45